T0195661

Welcome

ABOUT THE BOOK

If you are reading this, you or someone you know may be looking for help with a health problem. There are many books about healing, so choosing one can be challenging. I would like to be more helpful in your decision, but only you can feel whether this book is the right one for you. We have all been blessed with intuition, and your intuition may be more helpful in your decision than choosing a book solely on its credentials. An option is to take a moment—and take a couple of full breaths to settle yourself. Now, how does the book feel? In this moment, do you feel some Lightness? …Relief? …Strength? Do you feel it is attributable to the book?

Whatever you choose, I wish you the best in your search. If it is not this book, that is okay. I want you to find the healing process that brings you the most healing. And if this is not the one now, maybe it will be a better match for you later in life. After all, I do believe this book to be an acquired taste. The healing knowledge in this book has had a difficult history. I believe there were various times over the past three thousand years that this knowledge came to earth. Unfortunately, each time, much of the information was lost or concealed. This book is part of another attempt. My hope is humanity can embrace it this time and its full potential is realized forever.

BRIDGING THE GAP

VOLUME I: THOUGHTS, FEARS, REMEDIES, & HEALING

LEHS FIER; B. MOROV LLUV

BALBOA.PRESS
A DIVISION OF HAY HOUSE

Balboa Press books may be ordered through booksellers or by contacting:

Balboa Press
A Division of Hay House
1663 Liberty Drive
Bloomington, IN 47403
www.balboapress.com
844-682-1282

Print information available on the last page.

ISBN: 978-1-9822-7689-8 (sc)
ISBN: 978-1-9822-7691-1 (hc)

Library of Congress Control Number: 2021922820

Balboa Press rev. date: 12/22/2022

DEDICATION

The healing knowledge contained in these writings is dedicated to *you* and all of humanity. The knowledge of many healing remedies has been brought to humanity numerous times. And it has been an honor to be entrusted with healing knowledge so I could share it with all of you.

TABLE OF CONTENTS

ACKNOWLEDGMENTS

The first acknowledgment goes to the Divine. The source of all knowledge and love that is freely and continually given to humanity.

Another acknowledgment goes to my best friend. Her spiritual insightfulness revealed many of our experiences— experiences that we needed to acquire the knowledge for this book. We were able to partner our spiritual abilities in a special, unprecedented way.

Also, I acknowledge our friend Claudette, whom we found along the way. Her gifts as a person and her spiritual connection were gifts to us. Her ability to interpret information from the Divine surrounding these remedies helped us immensely in further understanding what we had been given.

Thanks to everyone who reviewed these remedies to ensure the most accurate information was presented to all of you. And thanks to all others who contributed in some way.

And thanks to all of you, the readers, who are willing to venture into a spiritual healing journey.

PREFACE I

The motivation for this book was to share healing knowledge with you that was inspired from the Divine. Some phrases used in these writings include "we were informed," "it is our understanding," "we have interpreted," and "we were asked." All these phrases were used to help delineate more specific information that we interpreted.

All exchanges of information have the potential for misunderstandings or misinterpretations. Therefore, several spiritually intuitive friends reviewed the material regarding the healing remedies to help ensure the accuracy of the interpreted information.

Over time, more knowledge will be revealed, which will allow this material to be viewed with a greater understanding, as learning is a continual process.

These writings also contain some of our experiential knowledge to help provide the reader with a greater understanding of the material. The main intent and purpose of this book is to make our interpreted information and our experiential knowledge available for your healing process—a process of healing accomplished between you and the Divine.

PREFACE II

Before January 2018, my focus in terms of the spiritual world was of love and light only. I knew dark or negative things existed, but I did not care to give my attention to them.

However, one evening, as I looked out of my window down a path in darkness, I envisioned one small, flickering flame in its way. At that moment, I acknowledged there was too much darkness in this world, and something needed to be done about it. Soon after that evening, my spiritual connections increased, along with an expansion of information. I did not understand *why.* What had changed? I was six months into this process when I recalled that *one evening*, and I realized that when I acknowledged that *something needed to be done with all this darkness*, the Divine must have interpreted that I was volunteering for the job. Now I understand why things had changed, and I am very grateful that I was included in this process, as it has been quite an honor and a special journey.

INTRODUCTION

An avid reader of healing books may read similar healing messages from many different legitimate intuitive authors. The reason the message sounds so similar is that many of these authors receive their information from basically one source.

The delivery of the information usually has a slightly different nuance, as the writings of each author are influenced by their personal experiences and perspectives. Everyone has their own way of learning, so a different presentation of similar healing information can provide readers with a different perspective, which can lead to a greater understanding.

Sometimes there is an expansion of information already out there or additional information that can help fill possible gaps or processes. This type of information can often be seen as a piece of the puzzle that further helps people understand their healing process. Each piece can help us in further seeing ourselves as a greater picture of health.

The healing information and the healing remedies revealed here are both a bridge and an expansion of a wonderful healing process. They are now made available to you for your healing journey with the Divine.

CHAPTER 1

THOUGHT

Our thoughts can greatly influence our perception of the world around us. By changing our thoughts, we can change our attitudes and behaviors. Thoughts can also influence our health. Healthier thoughts can be associated with greater well-being.

Our words echo our thoughts. Listen to the words you speak during the day. You may notice that your words, which are expressing your thoughts, may not be as *sound* or healthy as you once believed. When we put unhealthy thoughts to spoken word, we are actually reinforcing these unhealthy thoughts, thereby giving additional power to the unhealthy thought in our living experience. These unhealthy thoughts can be associated with our health problems.

Thought is the basic beginning of creation, so its involvement in your life is important. Examining our thoughts is often necessary since some unhealthy thoughts and our motivation to hold on to them are not easy to recognize. Sometimes we may have had them so long that we view them as being a normal part of our life, or they are deeply ingrained in our current belief system. Recognizing and understanding how our unhealthy thoughts affect our lives allows us to determine if they have any value for us. This critique helps us to release them and incorporate healthier thoughts that can create a more positive effect, including improved health.

If you are able to recognize an unhealthy thought before it becomes associated with a possible health problem, then good for you. Sometimes a health problem can be a notification that we need to make changes—changes to our thought processes and an awareness of what we have created around an unhealthy thought.

Recognizing unhealthy thought patterns and replacing them with correlating healthy thought patterns was made easier with Louise Hay's books. Her book *Heal Your Body* has a great reference guide to thought replacement, and it is highly recommended that you have this reference guide for part of the healing process described in this book. Louise Hay has provided us with a tremendous source of information.

CHAPTER 2

UNHEALTHY THOUGHTS TO FEARS

UNHEALTHY THOUGHT PATTERNS can lead to the creation of fears. Fears can be associated with many health issues—fears we created around our own unhealthy thought patterns.

A fear is created by us. We create fears to avoid things we think may cause us discomfort. The construction of a fear is part of our defense mechanism or protection to keep us away, or to prevent us, from experiencing unpleasant or painful feelings.

How do we manage to turn an unhealthy thought into a fear? To answer this question, I will use an example of the unhealthy thought of *not being good enough*. The negative emotions evoked from this thought may be small at first. Often, the emotion pops up when someone says something critical about us or our work. At first, the emotion we are likely to feel is irritation. This emotion is confirmation that we have a belief in the unhealthy thought of *not being good enough*. If we did not believe in this thought or if we viewed the thought with neutrality, we would not experience the negative emotion. As time continues, when we hear criticisms over and over, the level of irritation will likely increase. The negative energy of this emotion of irritation will reinforce and further solidify our belief in the unhealthy thought of *not being good enough*. The negative emotions are uncomfortable, and we will create a defense mechanism in attempt to avoid them. This defense mechanism is called a fear. Since criticism of us or our work is something that evokes the negative emotions we want to avoid, we will try to prevent our exposure to criticism.

At first, we may not perceive it as a fear until it gains more power. It gains its power in various ways but largely by the energy created in our negative emotional reactions. Over time, as the power of the fear grows, our irritations evoked from hearing criticisms can turn to anger. Anger has more energy than an irritation, so the fear grows as it uses this energy. Eventually, even the slightest criticism can get us highly agitated. As time passes, we may find ourselves in a state of more and more anger, and as a result, the fear grows more and more. We are creating a massive fear of criticism with the negative emotions evoked from the thought of *not being good enough.*

Often, the sensitivity can be heightened if the criticism comes from someone personally close to us, such as a family member. Knowing we will likely hear something critical from them that will result in us being angry, we are likely going to avoid them and others who we feel will be critical. We have become very sensitive because the fear has become so large and dominating. It is controlling our actions. Once we recognize our attempts to isolate ourselves from some people around us, our increasing anger, and the lower levels of energy we now experience, we may finally realize there is a health problem. In the example above, this person was experiencing feelings of *depression*.

Since the fear receives considerable energy from our negative emotions, such as anger, the fear can drain a person's energy and life force. Fears can negatively affect our lives and our relations with others. Fears also have the ability to interfere and block our connection with the Divine.

Never underestimate your creative abilities. You are a powerful creator. Unfortunately, fear creation is one of those abilities we all have. And since we are creators, we need to pay more attention to what we are creating. Otherwise, we may continue creating more fears based on unhealthy thoughts—fears that we provide energy to through negative emotions. In the spiritual realm, it is my interpretation that our fear creations can be viewed as a conscious energy. When we experience negative emotions because of an unhealthy thought, the energy of these emotions helps the fear grow energetically. The longer we stay stuck in an old unhealthy thought, the more the fear can grow. It is the perception of fears as *our created energy* of a fear that is referred to when discussing fears in this book.

♥

FEAR OR LOVE

I HEARD A LONG time ago that *fear* is the opposite of *love*. I did not understand that statement at the time. But now I understand, as fear and love will not co-exist in the same space. The understanding in this book is that many of our health problems are associated with fears—fears created by our unhealthy thoughts. In the book *Heal Your Body,* Louise Hay discusses releasing these unhealthy thoughts and replacing them with positive, loving affirmations. Removal of the unhealthy thought leads to the elimination of the fear from the body, and the loving affirmations help fill our body with unconditional love.

I commend the many people who have successfully mastered the technique of thought replacement outlined by Louise Hay. I purchased the book *Heal Your Body* many years ago to work on myself, but I struggled. I could recognize some of my unhealthy thought patterns, but it was difficult for me to let go of them. As a result, I had limited success. It was not the program; it was me.

Even though I struggled, I learned from the experience. I realized I needed something to help me remove unhealthy thought patterns—something to help me be more successful in thought replacement. I believed if I could reduce the power of the fear, it would help me in this process. So I turned my attention more toward the fear, knowing now its association with health problems and having the awareness of how overwhelming a powerful fear can become.

A fear can be quite dominant, making it difficult to focus on anything else. For instance, some fears can be associated with anxiety or panic attacks, and during this time, the focus is on surviving the episode. And even afterward, the mind can be overwhelmed with the fear of it happening again. Also, there are many situations where we can be overwhelmed with treating the symptoms of a health issue—a health issue associated with a fear.

If the fear was alleviated or eliminated, and the health problems with it, the unhealthy thought behind it could then be examined from a healthier perspective, thereby increasing the chances of successfully replacing unhealthy thoughts with positive affirmations.

However, how can we eliminate a fear before eliminating the unhealthy thought it was built around? The next chapters will discuss how and provide information we received to help with the healing process—information that helped me *bridge the gap* between removing old, unhealthy thoughts and their associated health problems and replacing them with new, positive thoughts and greater health.

RECEIVING THE REMEDIES

Over a period of approximately eighteen months, my best friend and I were put on a fast course of learning a spectrum of remedies. During this time, we were also made aware of many negative things. We referred to them as negative things or dark things, as we did not fully understand what they were.

During that time, the Divine provided us with a lot of experiences and a lot of knowledge. In the course of any given day, week, or month, a negative thing would be revealed to us. We would discuss the incident. My best friend is highly intuitive and was much better than I was at recognizing their presence. Sometimes it was more than just feeling the negative presence. We could also develop physical issues from its presence. Information acquired in these experiences was used to document its description and come up with the best possible reference name.

We needed a reference name to keep track of these things. A name was also appropriate, since the spirit world is often personified, and these things certainly had lives of their own.

The Divine was always consulted to ensure the reference name was the most suitable one.

After the name was established, we then asked the Divine what could be used to eliminate the negative thing we had encountered. Receiving the answer or solution for these negative things was a process. Sometimes we received an answer within hours, sometimes days, and sometimes a week. One solution took me more than three months because I originally did not correctly interpret the clues I was given. Many of the answers were given to us like clues or pieces of a puzzle and required us to put the different pieces together to get the full picture of the solution. It was an interesting endeavor for sure. It was special because each event was like a personal experience with the Divine and a collaborative partnership between the Divine, my best friend, and me.

Of course, we were pleased when we pieced together the information and established the necessary solution to eliminate the negative thing, especially when one of us was experiencing body pain, emotional pain, or some other health issue.

Once the correct solution was confirmed by the Divine, we would refer to the solution as the *remedy*. We would then say the following prayer—if it is the will of the Divine, to please send the *remedy* to the negative or dark thing to eliminate it. And then we thanked the Divine.

We found the remedies to be effective, and in some cases, we could feel the absence of this negative thing immediately. Sometimes, some physical effects experienced from their presence, particularly pain in the body or a rash, could take days or weeks to clear up. Most of the prayers were fulfilled quickly, but sometimes the prayer fulfillment was delayed, as certain events had to unfold first.

We accumulated an extensive list of reference names along with their remedies and some descriptions and symptoms. Eventually, our list consisted of approximately thirty-five remedies. There were many experiences, but it is not necessary to describe those events in any detail. The purpose was to provide some background information on how the knowledge of the remedies was received.

During those eighteen months, we were very fortunate to have a friend, Claudette, who has an amazing spiritual connection with the Divine. She was able to provide additional information regarding these remedies that helped us place these experiences in context. We had numerous meetings with her, and she was very helpful. It was during one of these meetings that the reference names and their descriptions I had written down were further addressed. She was informed that I was organizing or dissecting fears.

Previously, I had never thought of them in that manner. I had always referred to them as negative or dark things. I needed time after the meeting to understand them as fears. Interestingly, in the same session, our friend was also given the name Louise Hay.

These pieces of information would prove to be an important link to the type of knowledge we were receiving regarding these remedies. Soon after the meeting, I took out my book *Heal your Body* by Louise Hay. I could see the connection. Louise Hay often listed fear in her *probable cause* column of a health problem. Now I was able to accept the understanding that the negative or dark things we experienced were actually fears or fear things.

CHAPTER 5

FEAR AND FEAR REMEDIES

As DISCUSSED IN chapter 2, fears can be created from unhealthy thoughts. The remedies we were given can be used to eliminate the fears—fears that can be associated with health problems. The fear remedies can also help reduce the strength of the belief in the unhealthy thought associated with the fear. Removing the fear and reducing my belief in the unhealthy thought improved my success rate of removing unhealthy thoughts and replacing them with healthy, loving thoughts.

In the table of remedies, you may notice several remedies that may not be a part of your belief system. I have asked for possible substitutions for these remedies, but at this time, none have been given to me. If you are not comfortable with using a particular remedy, you may prefer to go directly to replacing the unhealthy thought with positive affirmations, as outlined by Louise Hay. When you successfully replace unhealthy thoughts with positive, loving thoughts, the fear will disappear from the body.

After a remedy is used, it is important to read chapter 9 and chapter 10. These chapters include additional steps that are necessary for this healing process, as well as important information from our experiences with the remedies.

Dealing with fears is important since we were informed that the majority of the human population has a number of fears. An important part of the healing journey brought forth in this book includes the use of fear remedies as part of a fear-removal process—removing fears that are associated with health problems and replacing them with love.

Since the remedies in this healing process are given as prayer remedies, the next chapter is devoted to some of the basic concepts involved in prayer.

CHAPTER 6

⬥

PRAYER

THIS CHAPTER WILL discuss some important features of prayer. In this discussion, it is important to note that *all is energy*. Our own spiritual body or essence is of energy, and some of these energy centers are embodied in our chakra system. Also, the essences of the remedies are also energy, and energy does not have the same constraints that physical remedies may have. It is energy that can be received by our spiritual essence from the Divine—energy that we can receive through prayer. Even prayer requests from us require a certain amount of energy. As a result, prayer involves an energy exchange between you and the Divine, and this energy exchange can be very much of love.

Some of the prayer methods that may hamper your success will now be discussed, as well as building blocks for more effective prayers. There may have been times when you felt that a prayer interaction or conversation was very one-sided. Like most relationships, good communication often needs more practice. Also, our view of a successful prayer may be hampered by a narrow view of what we are expecting to achieve from our prayer session, or we may have approached the prayer session with much skepticism. All of these can affect the effectiveness of a prayer.

The following are more points to consider when saying prayers. The Divine will not fulfill a prayer that would infringe on the free will of another individual. In my own prayers, I add the statement, "If it is the will of the Divine." This statement is not a reminder for the Divine but rather one's recognition that if a prayer infringes on another's free will, the prayer will not be fulfilled.

Sometimes prayers for healing are very general. Hopefully, we are more successful when using our expanded understanding of health issues in the body, as we now have more specific prayers to say to the Divine. In this way, we learn how to become part of our healing journey, as we follow the healing path step by step. Furthermore, once we understand this step-by-step template of healing, we can use this process if we encounter other health problems. We were informed this method of healing is duplicatable—a template that can be used by anyone and for different health issues.

The mental processes and our belief surrounding our prayer process are other important factors in our prayers being realized. If you say a prayer and are very doubtful it will be answered, then chances are you will receive that in return. In other words, it is doubtful you will experience your prayer being answered. Ironically, you will probably receive back what you sent, which was doubt.

When saying prayers, such as the prayers in this book, be *on notice* for thoughts of doubt that may arise. Doubts can negatively affect your thinking and your prayer requests. Doubt is not unusual, and I was informed to encourage you to please use the antidote of faith. You can ask the Divine for more faith as well.

It was mentioned earlier how we can take a thought and give power to it, especially through our emotions. However, a thought has very little power by itself. If we do not believe in a thought, then the thought has no power. Well, a prayer intention can be compared to a thought. By itself, a prayer intention does not carry a lot of power. However, if we focus on our intention and put it into spoken or written word, we begin to give it power. And like a thought, if we believe in it, then the prayer is empowered.

The amount of intent we put behind the prayer is what powers the prayer intention and is a significant factor in prayer manifestation. Also, the amount of intent placed behind the prayer increases the clarity of our intention and request. It is difficult for someone to give you what you want if you are not clear or keep changing your mind. Ask the parents who want to get a gift for their children, but the children change their mind every other day about what they want.

Also, we add more power to the prayer when we surround the prayer with positive emotions. An example is sending a loving, heartfelt prayer. Also, send the prayer with gratitude. Joy, peace, and contentment are also a wonderful presence surrounding your prayer but not a necessity.

I can't emphasize enough the value of a prayer sent in a loving, heartfelt manner. Love is the opposite of fear. And since many health issues can be associated with fears, a prayer to help you overcome this fear is most effective when offered with love, because in the end, your fear needs to be replaced with love.

Please never underestimate the power of prayer or the power of love. This whole healing process is based on the intent of replacing all unhealthy thoughts and fears with Divine Love—because love is the only thing that can truly heal us and our world.

CHAPTER 7

FEAR REMEDIES AND PRAYERS

IN THESE WRITINGS, I was informed to give you the instructions for the prayer format to administer the fear remedies. Chapter 6, "Prayers," was included in this book to help you through the prayer process. In the table of fear remedies, the prayer format is provided on numerous pages as a convenient reference. Each page has an example of an actual prayer to assist you in formulating these prayers and to help you become familiar with how to place the recommended remedy in the prayer format. Also, these remedies can be used in a meditation with the Divine if you are more comfortable with meditation. Ensure the remedy and the intent of eliminating the fear are incorporated in your spiritual connection. Both prayer and meditation are about interacting and connecting with the Divine.

Using prayer to apply the fear remedies serves multiple purposes. Through the spiritual gifts of our friend Claudette, we were informed that the world needs to turn to prayer because the world has lost conscious contact with the Divine. The following description was presented to us: "it is like a blanket of unawareness exists over humanity." Of course, this blanket of unawareness reflects the lack of conscious spiritual connections we currently have with the Divine.

We were also informed that the majority of the energy of the world's population is fear. Therefore, the fear or love scenario exists not only in our body, but it also exists on a larger scale in this world. Much of humanity has chosen to be in fear instead of being in love; we have chosen a world without conscious contact with the Divine and the love.

A path to Divine Love and the health it brings is through conscious contact with the Divine. Now we can see the Divine Wisdom requesting that we receive the healing energy of these remedies through prayer. The prayers can bring healing to our body by replacing fears with love, and in this process, we are making a conscious contact with the Divine. This conscious contact pierces through the blanket of unawareness, thereby bringing more of the Divine into our world. Since the Divine is love, our world becomes more loving and less fearful. Therefore, the prayer process results are twofold. It brings more love and healing to each of us and to all of the world.

CHAPTER 8

TABLE OF FEAR REMEDIES

In THE TABLE, some health problems involve two different fears. In this situation, it is acceptable to say the remedy prayer for each fear on the same day. As a result, both of them will be completed after three consecutive days. It is also acceptable to do one fear at a time—three consecutive days for the one fear, followed by another three consecutive days for the second fear.

Sometimes, two different fears can be associated with a similar health problem, but only one fear is involved. If you are able to determine which fear on your own, then you can say the remedy prayer for the fear you determined. If you are unsure, then it is best to say both prayer remedies.

Some health problems have three components as part of the remedy. In this case, all three components are placed in the space designated for the *Remedy* in the fear remedy prayer. Although there are three components, there is only one fear. A prayer example is provided in the table of fear remedies. One remedy has three components, and it is used differently because the fear actually has three distinct layers to it. A prayer example is also provided in the table.

When saying these prayers, remember the Divine has your best spiritual interests at heart. Make your intent very clear when saying these prayers, and know that the Divine will accommodate what is best for you. It is one of the perks of prayer over using the physical remedy.

A reminder that after the *fear remedy prayer* is completed, it is very important to refer to chapter 9 and chapter 10. These chapters include additional steps that are necessary in this healing process, as well as important information from some of our experiences with the remedies.

On numerous pages in the table, you will find a prayer format for you to use by placing the name of the health problem and the corresponding probable remedy in the blank spaces. Also, a prayer example is provided on each page to assist you in understanding how to use the prayer format. The health problem used in the prayer example on the page is denoted with an asterisk. The following is the basic prayer format used for the prayer remedies:

I ask the Divine to please send me the loving energy of _____to eliminate the fear associated with _____.

Remedy   Health Problem

Thanks be to the Divine."

Say this prayer once a day for three consecutive days.

Some health problems in the *table of fear remedies* are grouped together under one general health problem to simplify the table. Provided below are the names of health issues that are under a general name. The following is not the complete list of health problems in the table but only represents names included in a general health problem.

Health Problem	General Name in the Table
Alcoholism	Addictions
BPP vertigo	Balance (loss of)
Chicken pox	Herpesviruses
Cold sores	Herpesviruses
Cytomegalovirus	Herpesviruses
Classical distal RTA	Kidney issues
Colitis	Abdominal cramps
Dementia	Alzheimer's
Epstein-Barr	Herpesviruses
Genital herpes	Herpesviruses
Gonorrhea	Venereal infection
IBS, ileitis	Abdominal cramps
Labyrinthitis	Balance (loss of)
Meniere's	Balance (loss of)
Mononucleosis	Herpesviruses
Pyelonephritis	Kidney issues

Senility	Alzheimer's
Shingles	Herpesviruses
Sickle cell anemia	Anemia
Syphilis	Venereal infection
Vertigo	Balance (loss of)

TABLE OF FEAR REMEDIES

HEALTH PROBLEM	PROBABLE FEAR REMEDY
Abdominal Cramps (Colitis, ileitis, IBS)	1.Shiitake mushroom
Accidents	1.Frankincense oil
Addictions	1.Flower of bleeding hearts
AIDS/HIV	1.Convolvulus-A homeopathic 33x
Alzheimer's, Dementia*, Senility	1.Crystal of Moonstone, Crystal of Sunstone

*Prayer example:

I ask the Divine to please send me the loving energy of *Crystal of Moonstone and Crystal of Sunstone* to eliminate the fear associated with *Dementia*. Thanks be to the Divine.

Say this prayer once a day for three consecutive days.

Prayer Format:

I ask the Divine to please send me the loving energy of

_____ to eliminate the fear associated with _____.

Remedy   Health Problem

Thanks be to the Divine.

Say this prayer once a day for three consecutive days.

HEALTH PROBLEM	PROBABLE FEAR REMEDY
Amnesia*	1.Smelling salts
ALS	1.Peppermint oil
Anemia (and Sickle Cell)	1.Crab apple flower
Anxiety-regarding tasks	1.Crystal of Moonstone, Ashwagandha
regarding suffocation	1.Pure oxygen

*Prayer example:

I ask the Divine to please send me the loving energy of *Smelling salts* to eliminate the fear associated with *Amnesia*. Thanks be to the Divine.

Say this prayer once a day for three consecutive days.

Prayer Format:

I ask the Divine to please send me the loving energy of

_____ to eliminate the fear associated with _____.

  Remedy   Health Problem

Thanks be to the Divine.

Say this prayer once a day for three consecutive days.

HEALTH PROBLEM	PROBABLE FEAR REMEDY
Arteriosclerosis	1.Yellow star thistle
Arthritis (also see Rheumatoid)	1.Crab apple flower
Asphyxiating attacks*	1.Pure oxygen

*Prayer example:

I ask the Divine to please send me the loving energy of *Pure oxygen* to eliminate the fear associated with *Asphyxiating attacks*. Thanks be to the Divine.

Say this prayer once a day for three consecutive days.

Prayer Format:

I ask the Divine to please send me the loving energy of _____ to eliminate the fear associated with _____.

Remedy   Health Problem

Thanks be to the Divine.

Say this prayer once a day for three consecutive days.

HEALTH PROBLEM	PROBABLE FEAR REMEDY
Balance- Loss of	
Vertigo	1.Crystal of Moonstone
BPP Vertigo	1.Convolvulus-A homeopathic 33x
Labyrinthitis *	1.Sandalwood
Meniere's	1.Peppermint oil

*Prayer example:

I ask the Divine to please send me the loving energy of *Sandalwood* to eliminate the fear associated with *Labyrinthitis*. Thanks be to the Divine.

Say this prayer once a day for three consecutive days.

Prayer Format:

I ask the Divine to please send me the loving energy of

_____ to eliminate the fear associated with _____.

Remedy   Health Problem

Thanks be to the Divine.

Say this prayer once a day for three consecutive days.

HEALTH PROBLEM	PROBABLE FEAR REMEDY
Cancer*	1.Convolvulus-C homeopathic 3x, Bloodroot
Cardiomyopathy	1.Pure oxygen, Oak flower
Cerebral Palsy	1.Vibration of the Swooshing sound…
Conjunctivitis	1.Crab apple flower

*Prayer example:

I ask the Divine to please send me the loving energy of *Convolvulus-C homeopathic 3x and Bloodroot* to eliminate the fear associated with *Cancer*. Thanks be to the Divine.

Say this prayer once a day for three consecutive days.

Prayer Format:

I ask the Divine to please send me the loving energy of

_____ to eliminate the fear associated with _____.

Remedy   Health Problem

Thanks be to the Divine.

Say this prayer once a day for three consecutive days.

HEALTH PROBLEM	PROBABLE FEAR REMEDY
Cystic fibrosis * (1 fear, 3 layers)	1.a) Vascillious flower 1.b) Evening primrose flower 1.c) Blackberry flower Say the three following prayers on the same three consecutive days.

*Prayer :

I ask the Divine to please send me the loving energy of *Vascillious flower* to eliminate the fear associated with *Cystic fibrosis*. Thanks be to the Divine.

Say this prayer once a day for three consecutive days.

I ask the Divine to please send me the loving energy of *Evening primrose flower* to eliminate the fear associated with *Cystic fibrosis*. Thanks be to the Divine.

Say this prayer once a day for three consecutive days.

I ask the Divine to please send me the loving energy of *Blackberry flower* to eliminate the fear associated with *Cystic fibrosis*. Thanks be to the Divine.

Say this prayer once a day for three consecutive days.

HEALTH PROBLEM	PROBABLE FEAR REMEDY
Depression (2 possible fears)	1.the Belief that – "Life is a Gift" or 2.Crab apple flower Recommendation is that you send two remedy prayers since it could be the result of either fear. One prayer for each remedy.
Diabetes*	1.High Ultraviolet light

*Prayer example:

I ask the Divine to please send me the loving energy of *High Ultraviolet light* to eliminate the fear associated with *Diabetes*. Thanks be to the Divine.

Say this prayer once a day for three consecutive days.

Prayer Format:

I ask the Divine to please send me the loving energy of

_____ to eliminate the fear associated with _____.

  Remedy   Health Problem

Thanks be to the Divine.

Say this prayer once a day for three consecutive days.

HEALTH PROBLEM	PROBABLE FEAR REMEDY
Emphysema	1.Pure oxygen, Crystal of Yellow Topaz, Lemon oil
Epilepsy	1.Lavender oil
Gallstones	1.Garlic
Goiter*	1.Vibration of the Swooshing sound…

*Prayer example:

I ask the Divine to please send me the loving energy of *Vibration of the Swooshing sound…* to eliminate the fear associated with *Goiter*. Thanks be to the Divine.

Say this prayer once a day for three consecutive days.

Prayer Format:

I ask the Divine to please send me the loving energy of

_____ to eliminate the fear associated with _____.

   Remedy   Health Problem

Thanks be to the Divine.

Say this prayer once a day for three consecutive days.

HEALTH PROBLEM	PROBABLE FEAR REMEDY
Hepatitis*	
(A, B, D) - 1 fear	1.Galbanum oil
(C, E, F) - 2 fears	1. Galbanum oil 2. Peppermint oil For Hepatitis A, B, or D use Prayer 1 below. For Hepatitis C, E, or F use Prayer 1 and Prayer 2.

*Prayer 1:

I ask the Divine to please send me the loving energy of *Galbanum oil* to eliminate the fear associated with *Hepatitis*. Thanks be to the Divine.

Say this prayer once a day for three consecutive days.

----

*Prayer 2:

I ask the Divine to please send me the loving energy of *Peppermint oil* to eliminate the fear associated with *Hepatitis*. Thanks be to the Divine.

Say this prayer once a day for three consecutive days.

PROBLEM	PROBABLE FEAR REMEDY
Herpesviruses (Chicken Pox, Shingles*, etc.) (see list in Chapter 8)	1.Galbanum oil
Huntington's	1.Convolvulus-A homeopathic 33x
Kidney Stones	1.the Belief that – "Life is a Gift"

*Prayer example:

I ask the Divine to please send me the loving energy of *Galbanum oil* to eliminate the fear associated with *Shingles*. Thanks be to the Divine.

Say this prayer once a day for three consecutive days.

Prayer Format:

I ask the Divine to please send me the loving energy of

_____ to eliminate the fear associated with _____.

  Remedy   Health Problem

Thanks be to the Divine.

Say this prayer once a day for three consecutive days.

TABLE OF FEAR REMEDIES

PROBLEM	PROBABLE FEAR REMEDY
Kidney issues: (cont.)	
Classical Distal RTA	1.Blossom of the Moonflower vine
Pyelonephritis* (2 fears)	1.Crystal of Rose Quartz, Dandelions, Divine Light Crystal 2.Garlic The two required prayers for Pyelonephritis are given below.

*Prayer 1: example:
I ask the Divine to please send me the loving energy of *Crystal of Rose Quartz, Dandelions, and Divine Light Crystal* to eliminate the fear associated with *Pyelonephritis*. Thanks be to the Divine.

Say this prayer once a day for three consecutive days.
----
*Prayer 2: example:
I ask the Divine to please send me the loving energy of *Garlic* to eliminate the fear associated with *Pyelonephritis*.
Thanks be to the Divine.

Say this prayer once a day for three consecutive days.

HEALTH PROBLEM	PROBABLE FEAR REMEDY
Leprosy * (3 fears)	1.Garlic 2.Peppermint oil 3.Convolvulus-A homeopathic 33x Say the three following prayers for three consecutive days.

*Prayer :

I ask the Divine to please send me the loving energy of *Garlic* to eliminate the fear associated with *Leprosy*. Thanks be to the Divine.

Say this prayer once a day for three consecutive days.

I ask the Divine to please send me the loving energy of *Peppermint oil* to eliminate the fear associated with *Leprosy*. Thanks be to the Divine.

Say this prayer once a day for three consecutive days.

I ask the Divine to please send me the loving energy of *Convolvulus-A homeopathic 33x* to eliminate the fear associated with *Leprosy*. Thanks be to the Divine.

Say this prayer once a day for three consecutive days.

PROBLEM	PROBABLE FEAR REMEDY
Lupus (2 fears)	1.Peppermint oil 2.High Ultraviolet light
Migraine headaches*	1.Cypress oil
Multiple Sclerosis (2 fears)	1.Peppermint oil 2.Convolvulus-A homeopathic 33x
Parkinson's (2 fears)	1.Convolvulus-A homeopathic 33x 2.Crystal of Moonstone

*Prayer example:

I ask the Divine to please send me the loving energy of *Cypress oil* to eliminate the fear associated with *Migraine headaches*. Thanks be to the Divine.

Say this prayer once a day for three consecutive days.

Prayer Format:

I ask the Divine to please send me the loving energy of
_____ to eliminate the fear associated with _____.
   Remedy   Health Problem

Thanks be to the Divine.
Say this prayer once a day for three consecutive days.

HEALTH PROBLEM	PROBABLE FEAR REMEDY
Polio*	
Abortive -	1.Divine's warm soothing vibrational waves
Paralytic - (2 fears)	1.Divine's warm soothing vibrational waves 2.Peppermint oil
	For Abortive use Prayer 1 below. For Paralytic use Prayer 1 and Prayer 2

*Prayer 1:

I ask the Divine to please send me the loving energy of *Divine's warm soothing vibrational waves* to eliminate the fear associated with *Polio*. Thanks be to the Divine.

Say this prayer once a day for three consecutive days.

----

*Prayer 2:

I ask the Divine to please send me the loving energy of *Peppermint oil* to eliminate the fear associated with *Polio*. Thanks be to the Divine.

Say this prayer once a day for three consecutive days.

HEALTH PROBLEM	PROBABLE FEAR REMEDY
Rheumatoid* arthritis (2 fears)	1.Crab apple flower 2.Peppermint oil The two required prayers for Rheumatoid arthritis are given below.

*Prayer 1:

I ask the Divine to please send me the loving energy of *Crab apple flower* to eliminate the fear associated with *Rheumatoid arthritis*. Thanks be to the Divine.

Say this prayer once a day for three consecutive days.

----

*Prayer 2:

I ask the Divine to please send me the loving energy of *Peppermint oil* to eliminate the fear associated with *Rheumatoid arthritis*. Thanks be to the Divine.

Say this prayer once a day for three consecutive days.

HEALTH PROBLEM	PROBABLE FEAR REMEDY
Seizures	1.Lavender oil
Suicide- A* (deep despair, fear of dying)	1.the Belief in the Resurrection of Jesus Christ
Suicide- B (escape life, feeling very insecure)	1.Lion's mane fungi

*Prayer example:

I ask the Divine to please send me the loving energy of *the Belief in the Resurrection of Jesus Christ* to eliminate the fear associated with *Suicide*. Thanks be to the Divine.

Say this prayer once a day for three consecutive days.

Prayer Format:

I ask the Divine to please send me the loving energy of

_____ to eliminate the fear associated with _____.

Remedy   Health Problem

Thanks be to the Divine.

Say this prayer once a day for three consecutive days.

HEALTH PROBLEM	PROBABLE FEAR REMEDY
Tuberculosis	1.Pure oxygen, Pine oil
Venereal Infection (Gonorrhea, Syphilis*)	1.Blossom of the Moonflower vine

*Prayer example:

I ask the Divine to please send me the loving energy of *Blossom of the Moonflower vine* to eliminate the fear associated with *Syphilis*. Thanks be to the Divine.

Say this prayer once a day for three consecutive days.

Prayer Format:

I ask the Divine to please send me the loving energy of

_____ to eliminate the fear associated with _____.

   Remedy   Health Problem

Thanks be to the Divine.

Say this prayer once a day for three consecutive days.

CHAPTER 9

IMPORTANT STEPS AFTER REMEDY PRAYERS

THERE ARE MORE necessary steps required after the remedy prayers have been completed. These healing steps involve more prayers.

After a fear is removed, there is a space left in its absence. We were asked to fill this space with a nourisher. The nourisher is the Divine's Unconditional Love. I was asked to provide the following example of unconditional love. In those special moments when you bonded with your newborn baby, or when you bonded with a puppy or kitten, you may have experienced a deep feeling within your heart. It is a profound feeling that can bring tears of joy and love to your eyes as you deeply feel within you a pure love as you see them with no conditions. You see them only in innocence and perfection. Our spiritual essence is of love, and we were designed to flourish in the presence of pure, unconditional love. It is essential for our spiritual body, and it is the true nourisher.

The prayers in this book are designed to eliminate the fear and replenish our spiritual body with love. It is the energy of a fear, and not an unhealthy thought, that blocks or prevents the unconditional love of the Divine from flowing completely throughout us. It is the energy of a fear that interferes with the nourishment of Divine Love for our spiritual body because fear and love can't co-exist. Undernourishment of Divine Love in our spiritual body manifests itself in health problems of our physical being. It is synonymous with the undernourishment of our physical body with an inadequate food supply and its resulting health problems.

After completing the remedy prayer for removing the fear, ask the Divine to fill that empty space with Divine Unconditional Love. An example of such prayer is the following:

"I ask the Divine to please fill the space resulting from the elimination of the fear associated with_____ with Divine Unconditional Love.   Health Problem

Thanks be to the Divine."

This prayer for Divine Unconditional Love can be repeated daily or weekly for an extended period of time. You can determine your own duration of time. A prayer from a loving heart can help bring you into commune with the Divine. This exchange can create a greater flow of love and empower the prayer.

Shortly after I was introduced to the remedy prayers, I was informed that the remedy prayers can remove the fear from the body, but most of these remedies do not remove the fear from our world and humanity. To complete its elimination, we need to say another prayer, and it goes as follows:

"I ask the Divine to please send the King of kings with the iron sceptre to eliminate the fear associated with _____. Thanks be to the Divine."

Health Problem

This prayer allows the removal of the fear associated with the health problem from its existence in our world. Three years ago, I was directed to read some writings dating back about two thousand years. In those writings, it discussed the King of kings as one who is the defender of justice. My understanding is these fears are interfering with our free will, and as a result, they are in violation of a Divine Universal Law. However, the fear was our creation, and the Divine will not interfere with our free will. Therefore, by saying this prayer, we give the Divine the permission to eliminate our fear creation.

My best friend was shown the imagery of chains to represent fears. Fears are like chains that bind us and imprison our spiritual body. These chains (fears) restrain or interfere with our free will. She was also shown that by using the *fear remedies*, these chains can be broken, thereby restoring our free will. Our free will allows us to make decisions from a loving place, because free will—unlike fear—allows the presence and flow of love. On the other hand, fears block love and can control our actions and be both dominating and overwhelming. Often, fears keep us in fluctuating states of anger rather than in kindness and caring that come from love through free will.

After the remedy prayer and the two prayers discussed at the beginning of chapter 9 are completed, the final process involving thought replacement is next. You may have noticed some changes to your unhealthy thought. To complete the healing process, it needs to change. The fear remedy can reduce the strength in our belief of the unhealthy thought that we used to create the fear in the first place. Therefore, the final step involves the work provided by Louise Hay in her book *Heal Your Body*, which outlines her suggested steps for removing the unhealthy thought and replacing it with a healthy, positive, loving affirmation. The loving affirmations can continually bring more love for nourishment.

Even after completing the healing steps, the journey to better health continues, and it can take quite some time for complete physical healing. Some of the pathogens that were associated with this health problem can exist in the body for an extended period, even after the fear has been removed. The fear had been taking energy from the body and weakening the immune system. However, with the fear removed, the virulence of the pathogen should be reduced, and the body can begin to replenish its energy. The body should now have a greater opportunity to perform its healing powers. A healthier immune system should reduce the pathogens and their effects on the body.

The body will need to continue healing itself. The health issue may have been in the body for some time, and it may have taken a physical toll. The physical body needs to repair itself from the physical effects of the issue. Sometimes, the symptoms of the health problem can be the last to disappear, which can give a person the impression that nothing is changing.

The healing of the body will be different for everybody. Incorporating a healthier eating regime and a healthier lifestyle may help the body heal faster. For those interested in improving their eating regime for better health, an option is provided in a later section called "Further Reading."

The following is a summary of the steps in the healing journey discussed in this book:

1. Identify the health problem and match it up with the health problem in the *table of fear remedies*.

2. Use the corresponding *probable fear remedy* in a prayer. Repeat the remedy prayer for three consecutive days. Afterward, proceed to step 3.

3. Ask the Divine to fill the space resulting from the removal of the fear with the Divine's Unconditional Love.

4. Ask the Divine to send the King of kings to eliminate the fear, thereby eliminating the fear from our existence.

5. Match the original health problem to the same problem in the quick-reference guide supplied by Louise Hay in *Heal Your Body*.

6. Identify the unhealthy thought you believe was most likely associated with your health problem. Release the unhealthy thought.

7. Replace with a positive, loving affirmation supplied in the quick-reference guide by Louise Hay that you believe is best suited to your problem.

8. My suggested method of performing steps 5, 6, and 7 above is to follow the steps Louise Hay has outlined in the section "Further Comments" in her *Heal Your Body* book.

CHAPTER 10

FEAR REMEDY
EXPERIENTIAL KNOWLEDGE

THE FOLLOWING PROVIDES additional information regarding some of our own experiences working with the remedies.

Usually, there is only one of the same fear present. However, sometimes there can be several of the same type of fear. In this case, it is necessary to say a remedy prayer for three consecutive days for each fear. You need to deal with each fear one at a time, even though it is the same type of fear. After the removal of each fear, the prayer to fill that space with Divine Unconditional Love and the prayer for the King of kings need to be repeated. Several of the same type of fear may not be easy for you to determine. If you still feel the intensity of your fear after using the remedy prayer, then repeat the prayers.

Many people who have fears do not think they have them. Some fears can be subtle, or we may have had them for so long that we do not recognize them. Also, some fears do not fit the picture of how we view fears. Remember that they are our defense mechanism—our created protector to shield us. Often, emotional reactions are a good way to check for fears. One of the most prevalent emotions involved with fears is anger—including irritation, aggravation, frustration, and aggression. Another reaction is defensiveness. Since a fear is a defense mechanism, one can become quite defensive, and that may include anger. Most negative emotions are best to be examined, as they are often rooted in an unhealthy thought and based in a fear.

Two more items to address are guilt and resentment. It is my interpretation that these are also based in fears, so they are both blockers of love and separate us from the Divine. In terms of guilt, remember that you are often your harshest critic. It may not be easy, but forgiveness is key, and that includes forgiving yourself. Forgiveness is also the key to rid oneself of resentment. Resentment lacks an important aspect of love, which is compassion, and the lack of love provides proof that it is fear based.

Since both are fear based, both can be associated with health problems, as they negatively affect the presence and flow of love. The most probable fear for guilt and resentment is a fear I referenced as *judgment/condemnation*, and the fear remedy is the *blossom of the moonflower vine*. Use the remedy in the prayer format given in the table of fear remedies, and of course, follow it with the unconditional love prayer and the King of kings prayer. It is possible to have more than one guilt and more than one resentment. Once you have identified them, each guilt and each resentment requires its own set of prayers.

Also, we have noticed some involvement of fears in emotional blockages in the body, as well as other energy blockages; these energy blockages can be associated with pain and other problems. After removing the fear, a specialist in body energy work, such as a Reiki Master, can help in this health situation. Another option is a highly experiential healing modality for clearing emotional blockages known as breathwork. Researching the website of powerofbreath. com could be a good start to learn more about this healing method.

There are a couple of other options available when using the remedy prayers. If somehow the thought replacement is delayed, then it is advised to say the fear remedy prayer sequence again. Also, if the unhealthy thought still has more strength than you want to tackle with thought replacement, you can continue to say the fear remedy prayers for an extended period, until you are more comfortable with the thought-replacement exercise.

There will likely be more experiential knowledge acquired in the future, but the current list is all that we can address now.

Other health remedies in addition to the fear remedies were received, but the primary focus of this book is to provide you with fear remedies. Also, not all of the fear remedies are presented in this book. For easier learning and referencing, health problems that were not in the quick-reference guide supplied by Louise Hay were not included in this book. Also, there are numerous health problems in the quick-reference guide that are not covered in this book.

CHAPTER 11

ANOMALIES

We WERE INFORMED that many health problems involve fears. This chapter will discuss some health problems that may or may not involve fears.

Humanity has created many pollutants, and we have toxins in our air, land, and water sources, all of which can have a negative impact on our health. Heavy metals, chemicals, and other pollutants were items we had to address regarding our health situation. Since our environment is not pure, you can acquire heavy metals and chemicals numerous times in your lifetime. These pollutants and toxins in the body can play a part in many health issues, therefore, a resource on the topic of dealing with toxins in the body is provided in a section called "Additional Notes."

In addition to pollutants, health problems can be associated with mineral and vitamin deficiencies, such as deficiencies of zinc and vitamin D. Inadequate levels of vitamin D and absorbable zinc can be associated with an increased risk of viral infections and thyroid issues. Inadequate levels of vitamin D can also be associated with an increased risk of depression and SAD.

In a meeting with our friend Claudette, we were informed that a new wave of human-made health problems has already started. They called it *the frequency war.* We are bombarded daily by Wi-Fi, cell phones, EMF's, and other frequencies. Increased exposure and stronger frequencies, especially for those more sensitive to these frequencies, can be associated with health issues. Unfortunately, we were informed that 5G will considerably exacerbate these issues.

We have noticed in some health conditions that even after the health problem is gone, there can be some muscle memory symptoms that remain. We also came upon a situation where a significant pain was experienced in the solar plexus region that would appear every few months or so. It was assumed to be a digestion issue or pain caused by the gall bladder. It was a surprise when we realized that the cause of this pain originated in the third chakra. In this case, an appointment with a Reiki Master helped reduce the pain significantly. Shortly afterward, we learned about a naturopathic/homeopathic clinic that supplied homeopathic remedies for each chakra.

Not all of our unhealthy thoughts end up developing into fears, and there are situations where the unhealthy thought has not developed into a fear yet. There are health situations where the negative energy of an unhealthy thought has been associated with health issues; a few examples include some skin rashes, skin growths, and body aches.

We have been discussing how our unhealthy thoughts can have negative health effects on us. However, our unhealthy thoughts toward others can have unhealthy effects not only on ourselves but on others as well—more than one would expect. So please pay attention to your thoughts and do your best to replace unhealthy thoughts with healthy thoughts in all aspects of your life.

CHAPTER 12

♥

SUMMATION

THE HEALING JOURNEY presented in this book discusses a basis of many health problems and a path of healing. The understanding is that many health problems are based in a fear. We can create these fears from our unhealthy thoughts—unhealthy thoughts that come from our insecurities and doubts. Through various methods, we can provide this fear with energy, and it can become stronger. These fear creations take the space where love could reside, and eventually, these fears can be associated with health issues. The fear remedies can remove the fear from our body. Then the King of kings can eliminate this fear from our world upon our request. After the fear is removed from the body, this space can now be filled with the Divine's Unconditional Love—the true nourisher.

Next, we complete the cycle by replacing the original unhealthy thought with a loving, healthy, positive thought, thereby ensuring that the fear will not be recreated and further ensuring that only love resides in that space. As a result, we become more like our true essence of love, the loving spiritual beings we are intended to be.

The healing process described in this book not only helps *bridge the gap* in thought replacement but also helps *bridge the gap* between our world and Divine Love. Only Divine Love can truly transform our world—the eventual complete healing through the fulfillment of love.

CONCLUSION

A HEALING REVELATION

Our inner spirit or spiritual body began as pure love and in perfection like the Divine, and as a result, we also had the health these attributes provide. However, through negative experiences, misinformed messages, and inaccurate beliefs, we begin to think that our inner spirit is not in perfection. The example of an *imperfection* used in this book is the inaccurate thought of *not being good enough*. With inaccurate, unhealthy thoughts, we create fears, and this fear energy prevents and blocks love from being in those spaces of our spiritual essence. These fears inhibit our necessary nourishment of unconditional love. Therefore, for healing, we remove these fears with the use of *fear remedies*. We then continue the healing process with thought replacement, replacing thoughts of imperfection of our inner spirit with thoughts of perfection. In this healing way, the bookends are love. Complete love is where we all started, and after reinstating the original healthy, loving thoughts, we are then back to love and health.

As we battle with health problems and place our attention on disease pathogens, such as viruses and bacteria, it is easy to miss the bigger picture behind many health problems and the true underlying goal of the healing process. As we focus on the physical aspects of health regarding our physical body, we lose sight of the understanding that most health problems are a physical manifestation of our inner spirit that views itself as imperfect, and our view of these imperfections can be recognized in the form of our unhealthy thoughts.

Through the path of healing that was presented in these writings—eliminating fears and replacing them with love through loving thoughts—we are led to the true understanding of health problems and our complete healing, physically and spiritually.

The following is the underlying understanding in this spiritual healing process: "Our complete healing is accomplished through the fulfillment of Divine Love."

ADDITIONAL NOTES

The involvement of various pollutants, chemicals, and toxins in many current health issues was addressed extensively in the *Medical Medium* series by Anthony William, and he provides great healing solutions for overcoming these health issues. I highly recommend reading his material.

If the future allows for a volume II, it may contain information regarding not only remedies for fears but also for the pathogens left behind. By incorporating probable remedies for the pathogens, the body is likely to heal more quickly. The fear is addressed first. After the removal of the fear, it takes time for your body to heal. Remedies for the pathogens, reducing heavy metals and toxins, removal of unhealthy thoughts, a healthier lifestyle, and healthier food choices are all available tools for your body to attain greater health.

Prayers are incorporated into the healing process of this book, and I understand that for many of you, the use of prayers may take a leap of faith. As you increase your conscious contact with the Divine, you may become more comfortable with your requests and your personal relationship, so that you can commune daily with the Divine.

The following is an example of a prayer remedy protocol, which includes the probable pathogen remedy.

Health Problem: AIDS/HIV

Probable **Fear Remedy**: Convolvulus-A homeopathic 33x

Fear Remedy Prayer:

I ask the Divine to please send me the Loving energy of *Convolvulus-A homeopathic 33x* to eliminate the fear associated with *AIDS/HIV*. Thanks be to the Divine.

Say this prayer once a day for three consecutive days.

A fear remedy prayer using the remedy of the *Blossom of the Moonflower vine* in addition to the remedy prayer above is highly recommended.

After the three consecutive days, then say the following prayers:

I ask the Divine to please fill the current space resulting from the elimination of the fear associated with *AIDS/HIV* with the *Divine's Unconditional Love*. Thanks be to the Divine.

I ask the Divine to please send the *King of kings with the iron sceptre* to eliminate the fear associated with *AIDS/HIV*. Thanks be to the Divine.

Probable **Pathogen Remedy** associated with the fear: Gold, Frankincense, Myrrh.

I ask the Divine to please send me the Loving energy of *Gold, Frankincense, and Myrrh* to reduce/eliminate the pathogen(s) associated with *AIDS/HIV.* Thanks be to the Divine.

Say this prayer twice per day for ten consecutive days.

Also, after the fear remedy prayer is completed, do the thought-replacement technique outlined in Louise Hay's *Heal your Body* book. Refer to the section of "Further Comments" in Louise Hay's book for details.

FURTHER READING

INTERCONNECTIVITY—NOT ISOLATION

A multitude of health books are available. There is so much information, and even if it is good information, is it the best healing method for you? There are many different healing modalities, and each person may respond better to certain modalities than others. For some of the remedies in the table of fear remedies, sound healing therapy or light healing therapy would probably work. This is based on a statement made earlier, that *all is energy*, and because some of the remedies in this book include light and sound. Many healing modalities work with energy and frequency.

The diversity of health problems and the diversity of people have led me to believe there is no one author whose book alone is the only answer for everyone and for all health problems, including this book. That is one of the reasons there is a chapter dedicated to anomalies and this section on interconnectivity. Also, many different healing modalities have been mentioned in this book.

This book was not a book written in isolation. In the introduction, it was mentioned that we are all given pieces of the puzzle—pieces that help us get closer to seeing ourselves as a picture of health. These pieces include health information from a number of different authors. We were given knowledge about fears and fear remedies, and afterward, we were directed to Louise Hay's work. Explaining how fears are created involved the concept of unhealthy thoughts, and her books are a great resource for explaining unhealthy thoughts and thought replacement. Without thought replacement, the healing process described in this book would not be complete.

The interconnectivity of these writings does not stop with writings related to thought. There are more connections. In a previous chapter, it was mentioned that the body needs healing after the fear has been removed, and that it may be helpful to adopt a healthier eating regime. But which regime to pick? So many books propose their methods are the best. I read sections in the *Medical Medium* books by Anthony William, and I was impressed. The author not only outlines healthy foods to eat but also has a detailed knowledge of why those foods are important and pitfalls to watch out for in some food choices. Explanations are also provided for how substances and conditions in the body can promote pathogens and how foods can be used to eliminate them. His books are a great resource.

Interconnectivity can exist between seemingly very different healing modalities. When one reads Louise Hay's book *Heal Your Body,* referring to unhealthy thoughts and health issues, and then one reads Anthony William's book *Medical Medium: Liver Rescue*, referring to pathogens and health issues, it can be difficult to see their interconnectivity. The gap between the two methods could make them appear as two completely different healing modalities.

I do not see them as separate when using a bridge, and I can read them in general terms as one. Unhealthy thoughts can lead to the creation of fears. The fear creations are associated with health problems and their pathogens, such as viruses and bacteria. We are shown how pathogens function in the body and how conditions in the body make them more virulent. Remedies provided in this book can be used to reduce their virulence, and we are also shown how we can help our own body heal itself of pathogens and toxins through food and different life choices, and eventually, we will become more balanced and healthier again. In the end, I believe that for most health problems, the healing process is best completed by replacing the unhealthy thought that led us into this health problem.

In terms of health issues, we were informed that the association of fears with health problems and their pathogens, forms part of a bridge between the worlds of spirit and science. Energy and frequency are also part of the science world, and these attributes are found in many healing modalities, including the fear remedies. The worlds of spirit and science seemingly come from two completely different perspectives, yet as answers are revealed, they can complement each other.

COMMENTS

I was informed to write this book under a pen name, and currently, it is the recommended choice. There are numerous reasons for this decision, and one reason will be shared with you. In regard to the information in this book, the author is not the focus. The knowledge contained within the book is what is important, as well as its availability for your spiritual journey.

In a meeting with Claudette, we were informed that some people try to make an issue of the use of pen names and may resort to various forms of shaming. Interestingly, I was informed that a fear is the main motivation for shaming behavior. The following is the probable fear remedy prayer I was informed to provide:

"I ask the Divine to please send me the loving energy of the frequency of 633 MHz to eliminate the fear associated with shaming. Thanks be to the Divine."

Say this prayer once a day for three consecutive days.

If you are not able to recognize and replace the unhealthy thought from which this fear was created, then please continue using this remedy prayer for one month—and then whenever you feel it is necessary. This prayer can serve multiple situations. For example, you can say this prayer for an extended period if you are going through a time that is *unsettling* or you feel *unsettled*.

The pen names, like this book, were inspired by the Divine. For the readers who have grasped the underlying theme in the healing method that has been brought forth in this book, you will understand the wisdom in the pen names that were provided to me.

In chapter 7, it was mentioned that there are also worldly fears. If interested, below is a prayer to help reduce one of the more pervasive worldly fears.

> "If it is the Will of the Divine, I ask the Divine to please send the loving energy of Convolvulus-A homeopathic 33x to a pervasive worldly fear to reduce/eliminate this fear. I ask the Divine to please send the King of kings with the iron sceptre to reduce/eliminate this fear from our world. I ask the Divine to please fill the space resulting from the reduction/elimination of this fear with Divine Unconditional Love. Thanks be to the Divine."

FINAL NOTES

This section contains various notes that I would like to share with you about the book.

More than four years ago, when we began dealing with negative things and receiving remedies to eliminate them, we never imagined it would lead to writing a book about a healing process. During the process of discovering the remedy knowledge and writing it in this book, I was guided to the writings of two other authors. In order to present a more complete healing journey, it was beneficial to the readers to be directed to information provided by Louise Hay and information by Anthony William. The knowledge of the body and health that Anthony William shares is tremendous. His connection to Spirit is a blessing for all of us.

While writing this book, I was continually learning more about the healing journey. By the time the conclusion was written, I had gained new perspectives and a better understanding of the framework of this healing process, and I gained a whole new appreciation for the message Louise Hay brought to the healing process many years ago. She framed the healing process so well with her teachings on thought and love. She was very advanced in her knowledge of true healing. Her connection to the Divine Infinite Intelligence was also a blessing for all of us.

When I see the wonderful spiritual gifts of these writers, as well as those of my gifted friends, I am humbled by their spiritual abilities. I believe that the readers of this book also have interesting spiritual gifts. Some may not have recognized their gifts yet, while others are learning more about their own abilities. The diversity of gifts of each person helps make up our *wholeness*.

In this book, more than seven different healing modalities were mentioned. The choice of modality can be determined by the health issue at the time. A person in a car accident with physical trauma will likely seek a local hospital, whereas someone seeking help with a different health situation may incorporate other healing modalities. Several different modalities may be available for each different health situation, and they may not need to be mutually exclusive.

On a different note, no matter what medium format is used to present this information, each reader will have their own opinion of the best format. Unfortunately, at this time, these writings will not be available in e-form. We were informed that the power and energy of the word can't be maintained electronically in the same way as it can in print form in a book. As a result of this information, the book will be published in paper form only.

I truly hope that some of you have felt the pure energetic power and the loving intent of the Divine from which this book was written. Also, I hope readers find information in this book that will be helpful in their healing journey. This book is not large, so it is not *packed full*, but hopefully it can be *impactful*.

Although it is a small book, it carries a lot of important concepts—concepts I had the opportunity to absorb over a four-year period and experience along the way. Even now, when reading this book, I still find parts of it to sound bizarre. It is not an easy read. I certainly understand if some concepts are more than some of you want to believe at this time, and that is okay. I know how uncomfortable it can be when one's belief system is stretched. Sometimes it can help to leave it and come back to it later.

I am leaving a few last thoughts that I hope everyone can use in this lifetime:

Please never forget the immense love the Divine has for you, and remember this love is *unconditional*. Also, even though we come in different shapes, sizes, colors, and other differentiating features, we all come from One Source, and within all of us, we are all of the *same essence*, and this is our Oneness.

So, I encourage you to please be *kind* to *all* of humankind.

Thank You

ABOUT THE AUTHOR

I began discerning my vocation in life at the age of fourteen or fifteen. My vocational journey continued for seventeen to eighteen years. My journey required a close connection with the Divine in order to determine my calling in life. Since I felt a close connection with the Divine, I believed for many years, I was being lead to religious life. As the journey continued, I leaned more towards the single life as it seemed more flexible and would still allow me to focus my attention on the Divine. Towards the end of my vocational journey, I met someone and things changed. I was given the understanding from the Divine that I could be single if I so choose, but choose single life because it was something I wanted to do, and not because I believed it was something the Divine wanted me to do. It is all about free will. So my perspective of my vocational calling changed. However, my desire to grow my personal relationship with the Divine was still very important. When I was with the person I met, I felt even closer to the Divine. After many profound spiritual experiences at that time, I realized that sharing a life with this person was the best choice. I chose the vocation of marriage and that choice was a great surprise to me. I have realized my long vocational journey was a blessing in many ways, and the spiritual journey I share with my partner is confirmation that we have made a wonderful choice.

--- farmer ---

"As we focus on the physical aspects of health regarding our physical body, we lose sight of the understanding that most health problems are a physical manifestation of our inner spirit that views itself as imperfect, and our view of these imperfections can be recognized in the form of our unhealthy thoughts."

"We were designed to flourish in pure, unconditional love—it is essential for our spiritual body and is our true nourisher. And our complete healing is accomplished through the fulfillment of Divine Unconditional Love."

"Please never forget the immense love the Divine has for you and remember this love is *unconditional*. Also, even though we come in different shapes, colors, beliefs, and other differentiating features, we all come from One Source, and within all of us, we are all of the *same essence*, and this is our Oneness."

So, please be *kind* to *all* of humankind.

At times when you feel unsettled or circumstances around you are unsettling, the following prayer may be helpful:

"I ask the Divine to please send me the loving energy of the *frequency of 633 MHz* to eliminate the fear associated with feeling *unsettled*. Thanks be to the Divine."

This prayer can be repeated often and for an extended period of time. It is also recommended to use the prayer for the King of kings and the prayer for the Divine's Unconditional Love with this fear remedy prayer.

———◦———

Dis-ease can't thrive where there is no fear and no anger. If you are driven by fear, now may be the time to change driver.

———◦———

The fulfillment of Divine Love brings more healing, more health, more life, more joy, more love, and more peace. Love resolves all, it was designed that way.

Printed in the United States
by Baker & Taylor Publisher Services